Delicious SOUPS with HERBS

DAWN J. RANCK and
PHYLLIS PELLMAN GOOD

Good Books

Intercourse, PA 17534

Cover design and illustration by Cheryl Benner
Design by Dawn J. Ranck
Illustrations by Cheryl Benner

DELICIOUSLY EASY SOUPS WITH HERBS
Copyright © 1998 by Good Books, Intercourse, Pennsylvania, 17534
International Standard Book Number: 1-56148-255-2
Library of Congress Catalog Card Number: 98-41885

All rights reserved. Printed in the United States of America.
No part of this book may be reproduced in any manner,
except for brief quotations in critical articles or reviews, without permission.

Library of Congress Cataloging-in-Publication Data
Ranck, Dawn J.
    Deliciously easy soups with herbs / Dawn J. Ranck and
Phyllis Pellman Good.
    p. cm. -- (Deliciously easy -- with herbs)
ISBN 1-56148-255-2
1. Soups. 2. Cookery (Herbs) I. Good, Phyllis Pellman. II. Title.
III. Series: Ranck, Dawn J. Deliciously easy -- with herbs.
TX757.R46 1998
641.8'13--dc21   98-41885
                                                                    CIP

Table of Contents

Easy Multi-Bean Soup	4
White Bean Soup	5
Black Bean Soup	6
Mexican Black Bean Soup	7
Tomato Basil Soup	8
Basil-Tomato Soup	9
Tomato Soup with Lentils	10
Quick Tomato Soup	11
Hearty Vegetable Soup	12
Minestrone Soup	13
Hotch-Potch	14
Tim's Stew	15
Vegetarian Chili	16
Creamy Potato-Carrot Soup	17
Potato Soup	18
French Onion Soup	19
Essence of Mushroom Soup	20
Fresh Minted Pea Soup	21
Yogurt Mint Soup	21
Cool Cucumber Soup	22
French Sorrel Soup	23
Cream of Zucchini Basil Soup	24
Crab and Sage Bisque	25
Fish Chowder	26
New England Clam Chowder	27
Chicken Barley Soup	28
Japanese Noodle Soup	29
Autumn Bisque	30
Harvest Stew	31
Rosemary Stew	32
About the Authors	32

Easy Multi-Bean Soup

Davy Dabney
Dabney Herbs
Louisville, KY

Makes 16 servings

4 cups dry beans—a combination of Northern, navy, garbanzo, pinto, black, kidney, and/or lima, lentils and split peas, or use pkg. of bean soup mix
ham hock or 6-oz. can V8 juice
1/2 cup chopped onion
3 garlic cloves, minced
1/4 tsp. chopped fresh rosemary (1/8 tsp. dried)
15-oz. can tomato sauce
salt to taste
pepper to taste
crushed jalapeno pepper (optional)

1. Soak beans overnight in 4 quarts water. In the morning, add ham hock or V8 juice to the beans and soaking water. Cover and simmer for 2-2 1/2 hours, or until beans and ham hock are tender.
2. Stir in onion, garlic, rosemary, and tomato sauce. Cover and simmer until onions are tender.
3. Season with salt, pepper, and jalapeno before serving.

Tip for Using Herbs

Dawn Ranck
Harrisonburg, VA

Before beginning to cook a meal, I cut bunches of herbs from my herb garden and arrange them in a vase on my counter. I can then clip off the herbs I need for cooking and for decorating my food. The remaining herbs make a nice bouquet to brighten up the kitchen.

White Bean Soup

Barbara Warren
Provincial Herbs
Folsom, PA

Makes 12 servings

1 lb. dry cannellini beans or
    48 oz. canned beans
3 oz. prosciutto or bacon
4 oz. carrots, diced
8 oz. red onion, diced
1 bay leaf

1 Tbsp. fresh rosemary
3 qts. chicken stock
salt to taste
pepper to taste
fresh sprig of rosemary

1. Soak dry beans overnight in water to soften. Use 4 cups water to 1 cup dry beans. Bring beans to boil in water in which they have soaked, cover soup pot, and simmer 2 to 3 hours, or until beans are tender but not mushy.
2. In large stockpot, saute prosciutto until fat is rendered. Stir in carrots, onions, bay leaf, and rosemary. Cook until soft.
3. Add beans and stock. Simmer until heated through.
4. Season with salt and pepper.
5. Garnish with a sprig of rosemary before serving.

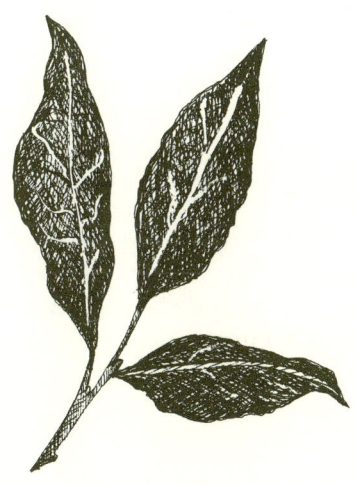

Black Bean Soup

James O'Toole
O'Toole's Herb Farm
Madison, FL

Makes 8 servings

1 lb. dry black beans
10 cups water
1 large bell pepper, quartered, with seeds removed
1 large onion, chopped fine
1 large bell pepper, chopped fine
6 large garlic cloves, minced
2 Tbsp. extra virgin olive oil
3 tsp. salt
1 tsp. pepper
1 1/2 tsp. chopped fresh oregano (1/2 tsp. dried)
1/2 cup green olives with pimento, cut in half
1 bay leaf
1 1/2 tsp. sugar
4 Tbsp. juice from olive jar
2 Tbsp. red wine
half a large onion, chopped fine
half a bell pepper, chopped
fresh cilantro to taste
1/3 cup extra virgin olive oil, if desired

1. Wash beans. Cover beans with water and soak with one quartered bell pepper overnight.
2. Cook in soaking water for 1 1/2 hours over medium heat, stirring occasionally, adding water if necessary, until beans are soft.
3. Saute onion, 1 chopped bell pepper, and garlic in 2 Tbsp. oil until soft. Add 1 cup softened beans and mash mixture.
4. Stir in salt, pepper, oregano, olives, bay leaf, and sugar. Allow to boil over low heat for 1 hour.
5. Add juice from olives and wine. Cook over low heat for an additional 20 minutes, or until soup has reached desired thickness.
6. Combine remaining finely chopped onion, bell pepper, and cilantro.
7. Remove soup from heat and remove bay leaf.
8. Pass the chopped onion, pepper, and cilantro to the diners to add to their individual soup bowls. Pass the olive oil so that each may drizzle oil over their soup, if they wish.

Mexican Black Bean Soup

Carolee Snyder
Carolee's Herb Farm
Hartford City, IN

Makes 6 servings

1 cup diced onion
1 cup chopped carrots
1 cup diced celery
1 clove garlic, minced

1 Tbsp. oil
2 15-oz. cans black beans
¾ cup water
2 Tbsp. mild taco sauce

Salsa:
4 plum tomatoes
6 tomatillos
¼ cup chopped onion
juice of lime
dash of salt

1 jalapeno pepper,
   finely chopped
½ cup chopped fresh
   cilantro

sour cream, optional

1. Saute onion, carrots, celery, and garlic in oil until tender.
2. Stir in beans, water, and taco sauce. Cover and simmer, stirring occasionally, for 30-45 minutes.
3. Place tomatoes, tomatillos, and onion in food processor. Chop coarsely. Add lime juice, salt, jalapeno, and cilantro. Mix well. Chill.
4. Dip soup into bowls. Place a spoonful of salsa and a spoonful of sour cream on top of each bowl.

Tomato Basil Soup

Janet Melvin
Heritage Restaurant Gardens and Gifts
Cincinnati, OH

Makes 12 servings

2 Tbsp. butter or margarine
1/2 cup diced onion
1 Tbsp. minced garlic
2 cups chicken stock
2 28-oz. cans crushed tomatoes
2 cups heavy cream
1/4 cup chopped fresh basil
1 Tbsp. salt
1 1/2 tsp. white pepper
chopped fresh basiL

1. Saute onions in butter until transparent.
2. Add garlic and saute for 1 minute.
3. Stir in remaining ingredients, and heat through. Make sure consistency of the soup is only a little thicker than heavy cream. If the soup is too thick, thin with half-and-half.
4. Serve hot with chopped fresh basil on top as garnish.

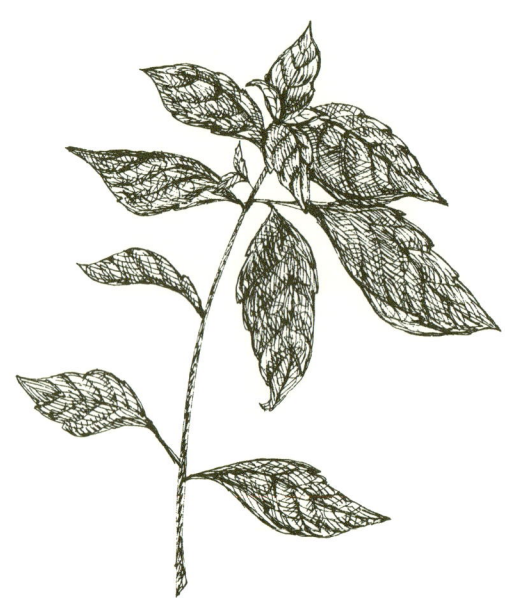

Basil-Tomato Soup

Sandie Shores
Herbs' Herbs and Such . . .
Rochester, MN

Makes 6 servings

3 Tbsp. butter	¾ cup sugar
1 large carrot, shredded	½ cup lightly packed fresh basil leaves, chopped
1 large onion, chopped	
4 large ripe tomatoes, peeled, seeded, and chopped	14½-oz. can chicken broth
	salt to taste
⅛ tsp. pepper	chopped parsley for garnish

1. Melt butter in 3-quart saucepan over medium heat. Stir in carrot and onion. Cook, stirring often, until onion is slightly soft.
2. Stir in tomatoes, pepper, sugar, and half of basil. Bring to boil, stirring to prevent sticking. Reduce heat. Cover and simmer for 15 minutes.
3. In blender or food processor, whirl the tomato mixture, a portion at a time, until smooth.
4. Return mixture to saucepan over medium heat. Stir in chicken broth, remaining basil, and salt. Heat.
5. Serve, garnished with parsley.

Tip for Storing Fresh Herbs

Lewis J. Matt III
White Buck Farm
Holbrook, PA

Fresh herb leaves can be stored for a long time if moistened and placed in an inflated plastic bag in the lower part of the refrigerator. Every day shake the bag, wipe out excess moisture, and reinflate the bag. The bag should never be more than half full of leaves and should be filled with as much air as possible.

Tomato Soup with Lentils

Anne Walker
Sweet Annie Herbs
Centre Hall, PA

Makes 6 servings

½ cup dried lentils
1 clove garlic, minced
¼ tsp. black pepper
2 Tbsp. extra virgin olive oil
4 medium tomatoes, cubed
1 medium green pepper, chopped
3 Tbsp. chopped fresh parsley (1 Tbsp. dried)

1½ Tbsp. chopped fresh oregano (½ Tbsp. dried)
1 tsp. ground coriander
8 cups vegetable stock
1 Tbsp. tomato paste
1 tsp. brown sugar
pinch of cayenne pepper
salt to taste
1 Tbsp. burgundy

1. Cover lentils with water and simmer for 45 minutes. Set aside.
2. Saute garlic and black pepper in oil for 4-6 minutes. Stir in tomatoes and simmer for 20 minutes.
3. Stir in green pepper, parsley, oregano, coriander, and stock. Bring to boil. Lower heat and simmer until slightly reduced, about 30 minutes.
4. Drain lentils and add to soup.
5. Stir in remaining ingredients and continue to simmer for 20-30 minutes, stirring frequently.

Tip for Using Herbs

Barb Perry
Lizard Lick Organic Herbs
Huron, TN

The primary rule for cooking with herbs is: let your taste buds be your guide. Using herbs is limited only by the imagination of the person who is cooking! When sprinkling herbs on a dish, if it looks like too much, it is probably just right!

Quick Tomato Soup

Peggy Ritchie
Herbs and More
Ocala, FL

Makes 4-6 servings

- 2 Tbsp. butter or margarine
- 4 Tbsp. flour
- 3 cups chicken stock
- 3 cups home-canned tomato or V8 juice
- 3 large fresh tomatoes, peeled and diced
- 1 cup cooked rice
- 1/2 tsp. coriander
- 3 Tbsp. chopped fresh dill (1 Tbsp. dried)
- 1 Tbsp. raspberry vinegar, or vinegar of your choice
- Parmesan cheese

1. Mix together butter and flour. Brown.
2. Add stock, stirring constantly.
3. Stir in juice and tomatoes. Bring to boil. Reduce heat and simmer for 5-10 minutes.
4. Stir in rice, coriander, dill, and vinegar. Serve hot, sprinkled with Parmesan cheese.

Hearty Vegetable Soup

Sheryl Lozier
Summers Past Farms
El Cajon, CA

Makes 5-6 servings

- 1/2 cup diced onion
- 2 cloves garlic, minced
- 1/2 cup diced leek
- 1/2 cup diced celery
- 1/2 cup diced cabbage
- 1/2 cup diced carrot
- 8 Tbsp. butter
- 2 tsp. chopped fresh thyme (2/3 tsp. dried)
- 2 bay leaves
- 2 tsp. tomato paste
- 1 1/2 qts. vegetable stock
- 1/4 cup corn kernels
- 1/4 cup shredded spinach
- 1/4 cup sliced mushrooms
- 2 Tbsp. grated Asiago cheese
- 2 tomatoes, diced
- 12 oz. poached chicken breast, diced
- 2 tsp. chopped fresh parsley (2/3 tsp. dried)

1. In stockpot, mix together onion, garlic, leek, celery, cabbage, carrot, and butter. Cover with lid and cook for 2-3 minutes, being careful not to brown vegetables while cooking.
2. Stir in thyme, bay leaves, tomato paste, and vegetable stock. Simmer for 20 minutes.
3. Stir in corn, spinach, and mushrooms. Simmer for 3 minutes.
4. Remove soup from stove. Skim if necessary.
5. Ladle soup into warm soup bowls. Garnish with cheese, tomatoes, chicken, and parsley.

Minestrone Soup

Connie Johnson
Heartstone Herb Farm
Loudon, NH

Makes 6-8 servings

3 Tbsp. olive oil
2 large onions, chopped
4 garlic cloves, crushed
2 qts. chicken broth
1-lb. can tomatoes
1 cup shredded cabbage
2 large carrots, sliced
2 bay leaves
cayenne pepper to taste
3 tsp. chopped fresh basil ($1/2$ tsp. dried)
2 Tbsp. chopped fresh parsley (2 tsp. dried)
2 stalks fresh lovage
1-lb. can garbanzo beans
1-lb. can kidney beans
1 cup cooked pasta
grated cheese

1. In large saucepan, saute onions and garlic in oil. Cook until onions are transparent.
2. Add broth, tomatoes, cabbage, carrots, bay leaves, cayenne pepper, basil, and parsley. Cook until vegetables are tender.
3. Stir in lovage, garbanzo beans, kidney beans, and pasta. Simmer for 10 minutes.
4. Sprinkle with grated cheese and serve.

Hotch-Potch

Helen N. Lamb
Lavender Hill Herb Farm
Hockessin, DE

Makes 4-6 servings

2 cups young vegetables (carrots, turnips, cauliflower, or any combination you prefer), diced
2 quarts water or chicken broth
half a head of lettuce, shredded
1 cup fresh green peas
1 cup fresh lima beans
2-4 scallions, chopped
¼ cup chopped fresh parsley (5 tsp. dried)
1 Tbsp. chopped fresh thyme (1 tsp. dried)
1 Tbsp. chopped fresh savory (1 tsp. dried)
1 tsp. salt
¼ tsp. pepper
1 tsp. sugar

1. Place carrots, turnips, and cauliflower in water or broth. Simmer until tender.
2. Add lettuce, peas, lima beans, and scallions. Cook another 10 minutes.
3. Before serving, add parsley, thyme, savory, salt, pepper, and sugar. Heat to piping hot.

Tip for Using Herbs

Marian E. Sebastiano
Salt Box Gallery Herbs
Hubbard, OH

To learn the individual flavor of an herb, finely chop a few teaspoons of it and mix it with a bland base such as sour cream, cream cheese, butter, or plain yogurt. Let the mixture set in the refrigerator for several hours. Use as a dip or spread for raw vegetables, bread, or crackers.

Tim's Stew

Tim Brown
Full Circle Farm
Rockford, TN

Makes 8-10 servings

3 cans whole kernel corn
5-6 large potatoes, diced
3 large yellow onions, chopped
4-5 cloves garlic, minced
2-3 dashes black pepper
2-3 dashes red pepper

2 cups water
8 oz. sliced or shredded sharp cheddar cheese
soy sauce to taste
3/4 tsp. chopped fresh thyme (1/4 tsp. dried)

1. Drain corn juice into large pot. Add potatoes, onions, garlic, and peppers. Add water. Simmer until potatoes are tender, 30-40 minutes.
2. Stir in corn, cheese, and soy sauce. Heat until cheese is melted.
3. Garnish with thyme and serve.

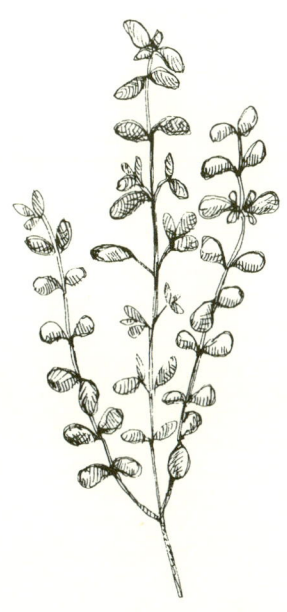

Vegetarian Chili

Nancy Ketner
Sweet Earth
West Reading, PA

Makes 8-10 servings

- 1/4 cup olive oil
- 1/3 cup tamari soy sauce
- 2 tsp. chili powder
- 1 Tbsp. cumin
- 1 lb. tofu, cut into 3/4" cubes
- 1 onion, diced
- 1 tsp. minced garlic
- 4 Tbsp. olive oil
- 1/2 tsp. mustard seeds
- 15-oz. can red kidney beans, drained, liquid reserved
- 19-oz. can black beans, drained, liquid reserved
- 20-oz. can crushed plum tomatoes
- 1/2 cup chopped fresh cilantro
- 2 Tbsp. chopped fresh basil
- 1 tsp. cayenne pepper

1. Mix together 1/4 cup olive oil, soy sauce, chili powder, and cumin. Pour over tofu and marinate for 30 minutes.
2. In skillet saute onion and garlic in 4 Tbsp. olive oil. Stir in mustard seeds.
3. Remove tofu from marinade with slotted spoon. Add to skillet. Saute for 10 minutes, until all sides are brown.
4. In a slow cooker, combine marinade, tofu-onion mixture, beans, tomatoes, cilantro, basil, cayenne, and enough bean liquid to just cover the ingredients.
5. Cook on low for at least 6 hours. Remove lid to thicken if desired.

Creamy Potato-Carrot Soup

Barbara Corrales
Honeysuckle Farm Herbs
Lafayette, LA

Makes 6-8 servings

1 large onion, chopped
1/2 cup chopped celery
3-5 cloves fresh garlic, minced
1 Tbsp. oil
6 carrots, chopped or sliced
2 medium potatoes, peeled and chopped or sliced
2 14 1/2-oz. cans chicken broth
1/3 cup fresh parsley (5 tsp. dried)
2 Tbsp. fresh lemon thyme (2 tsp. dried)
1 tsp. ground cumin
1/4-1/2 tsp. cayenne or black pepper, or combination
1/2-1 cup evaporated milk skim or regular
salt to taste
finely sliced chives

1. In large kettle, saute onion, celery, and garlic in oil until onion wilts, about 5 minutes.
2. Add chopped or sliced carrots and potatoes, chicken broth, parsley, lemon thyme, cumin, and pepper. Bring to boil. Reduce heat to medium-low. Cover and cook until vegetables are fork-tender, approximately 20 minutes. Remove from heat and cool enough to process vegetables in food processor or blender.
3. Puree soup in small batches. Return to kettle.
4. Add milk until desired consistency is reached. Season with salt. Heat to simmering on low heat.
5. Garnish with sliced chives just before serving.

Potato Soup

Marian E. Sebastiano
Salt Box Gallery Herbs
Hubbard, OH

Makes 8 servings

4 strips bacon, diced
2 cloves garlic
1/2 cup chopped onion
1 celery stalk chopped,
 or 1/4 tsp. celery salt
8 medium-sized potatoes,
 peeled and cubed
bay leaf

1 1/2" thick piece of
 Velveeta cheese
1 cup milk
salt to taste
pepper to taste
parsley leaves,
 or chopped fresh dill

1. Saute bacon until pan is coated with drippings.
2. Add garlic, onion, and celery. Saute until onion is transparent and bacon is still soft.
3. Add potatoes and bay leaf. Cover with water. Cook until potatoes test soft, about 15 minutes.
4. Mash potatoes or puree in a blender.
5. Stir in cheese, milk, salt, and pepper. Bring to boiling point.
6. Sprinkle with parsley or dill before serving.

Tip for Using Herbs

Diane Tracey
Chestnut Herb Farm
North Ridgeville, OH

Replenish dried herbs for cooking yearly. Use old herbs in the bath as bath herbs. The heat from the water will release remaining oils in the herbs.

French Onion Soup

Linda Kosa-Postl
Never Enough Thyme
Granite Fall, WA

Makes 4 servings

3 Tbsp. butter or margarine
1 Tbsp. olive oil
4-5 cups thinly sliced onions
1 tsp. salt
1/2 tsp. sugar
3 Tbsp. flour
6 cups beef bouillon

3 cups light red wine
1 bay leaf
1 1/2 tsp. chopped fresh thyme (1/2 tsp. dried)
salt to taste
pepper to taste

1. Cook onions in butter and olive oil over low heat for 15-20 minutes, covered, stirring occasionally.
2. Uncover and raise heat to medium. Stir in salt and sugar. Cook for 30 minutes, stirring frequently, until onions turn a golden brown.
3. Lower heat. Stir in flour to make a paste.
4. Add bouillon, wine, bay leaf, and thyme. Simmer for 20-30 minutes. Season with salt and pepper.

Variation: Use white wine instead of red wine for a more delicate taste.

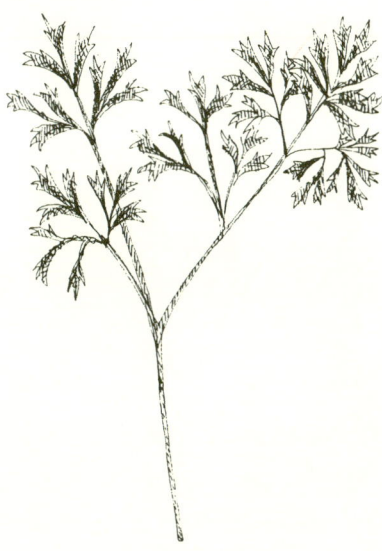

Essence of Mushroom Soup

Judy Kehs
Cricket Hill Herb Farm
Rowley, MA

Makes 6-8 servings

- 1/2 lb. fresh mushrooms, or 14-oz. canned
- 1 carrot, cut in small chunks
- 1 stalk celery, chopped, or 4 4"-sprigs of fresh lovage, chopped
- 2 Tbsp. chopped fresh parsley (2 tsp. dried)
- 2 tsp. chopped fresh tarragon (2/3 tsp. dried)
- 2 tsp. chopped fresh thyme (2/3 tsp dried)
- 1/2 cup water
- 10 oz. chicken broth
- 4 Tbsp. Madeira wine
- sour cream for garnish

1. Cook mushrooms, carrot, celery, parsley, tarragon, and thyme in water until soft.
2. In blender, mix together vegetables and chicken broth. Blend until smooth. Return to pan and reheat.
3. Stir in Madeira. Serve garnished with dollop of sour cream.

Variation: *Add slivers of fresh mushrooms, freshly grated provolone cheese, and a dash of white pepper as garnishes.*

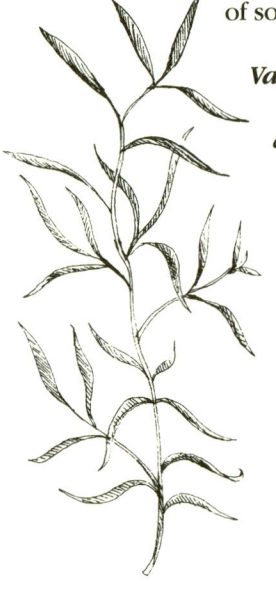

Fresh Minted Pea Soup

Ary Bruno
Koinonia Farm
Stevenson, MD

Makes 8 servings

3 cups fresh shelled peas
2 Tbsp. chopped fresh chives
1 tsp. chopped fresh mint
1 tsp. chopped fresh
   thyme leaves

4 Tbsp. chopped fresh
   Italian parsley
4 cups chicken stock
sea salt to taste

1. Process the peas, herbs, and 1 cup of stock in a blender until smooth.
2. Heat the rest of the stock to boiling. Stir in pea mixture.
3. Heat to simmer. Cook gently for 4-5 minutes. Salt and serve.

Variation: *For a cream soup, substitute 1/2 cup heavy cream for 1 cup of stock. Add cream just before serving.*

Yogurt Mint Soup

Gerry Janus
Vileniki—An Herb Farm
Montdale, PA

Makes 5 servings

2 cups plain yogurt
1 small cucumber, chopped
1/4 tsp. salt
dash of freshly ground pepper
2 Tbsp. chopped fresh
   mint leaves

3 Tbsp. chopped mint
   blossoms
mint blossoms

1. Place yogurt, cucumber, salt, and pepper in food processor or blender and process until smooth.
2. Stir in chopped mint and blossoms. Chill for at least 2 hours.
3. Garnish with additional mint blossoms just before serving.

Cool Cucumber Soup

Mark Silber
Hedgehog Hill Farm
Sumner, ME

Makes 4 servings

2 medium-sized cucumbers
1 cup buttermilk
1/4 cup chopped fresh parsley
2 tsp. chopped fresh chives
1 1/2 tsp. chopped fresh dill
 (1/2 tsp. dried)
6 fresh mint leaves
 (1/4 tsp. dried)
1/4 tsp. chopped fresh tarragon (1/8 tsp. dried)
2 tsp. lemon juice
1 1/2 cups yogurt
3 Tbsp. chopped fresh dill and mint leaves, combined

1. Peel cucumbers. Cut in half lengthwise and scoop out seeds. Cut flesh into chunks.
2. Place cucumbers, buttermilk, parsley, chives, dill, mint, tarragon, and lemon juice in blender. Blend until smooth and then transfer to a bowl.
3. Whisk in yogurt. Chill.
4. Sprinkle with dill and mint leaves before serving.

French Sorrel Soup

Janette Petersen
The Rose Herb Nursery
La Center, CO

Makes 4 servings

2 Tbsp. butter	2 Tbsp. flour
1 medium onion, chopped	2 cups chicken or vegetable stock
4 Tbsp. chopped fresh lovage leaves (4 tsp. dried)	1 cup milk
4 Tbsp. chopped fresh French sorrel leaves (4 tsp. dried)	salt to taste
	pepper to taste

1. Saute onion in butter for 5 minutes, or until onions are soft.
2. Stir in lovage and French sorrel.
3. Stir in flour and cook for 1 minute, stirring constantly.
4. Gradually stir in stock. Cover and simmer gently for 15 minutes.
5. Stir in milk, salt, and pepper. Reheat slowly. Do not boil.

Tip for Growing Herbs

Linda Jani & Chris Aylesworth
Viewhurst Farm Herb & Garden Shop
Hebron, IN

Locating your kitchen garden close to your back door or close to the kitchen is essential. If you can't easily slip out and cut fresh herbs, you won't use them as much or as often.

Cream of Zucchini Basil Soup

Debbie Tissot
Cottage Herbs
Albuquerque, NM

Makes 2 quarts

6-8 zucchini, chopped into 3/4" chunks
3-5 chicken bouillon cubes
1 large onion, chopped
3 Tbsp. butter or margarine
2 cloves garlic, minced
1/4-1/2 cup chopped fresh basil (1 1/2-3 Tbsp. dried)
1 Tbsp. chopped fresh tarragon (1 tsp. dried)
2 Tbsp. chopped fresh parsley (2 tsp. dried)
8 oz. cream cheese
freshly ground pepper to taste
salt to taste

1. In large kettle, mix together zucchini and bouillon cubes. Cover with water and bring to a boil.
2. Saute onion in butter until transparent. Add garlic and saute for several minutes. Stir into zucchini mixture.
3. Stir in basil, tarragon, and parsley. Reduce heat and simmer for 10 minutes.
4. In blender or food processor, mix together a portion of soup and half the cream cheese. Blend until smooth. Add rest of cream cheese and blend until smooth. Return to pot and stir until cream cheese is dissolved.
5. Season with salt and pepper.

Tip for Harvesting Herbs

Tim Brown
Full Circle Farm
Rockford, TN

Harvest herbs after the dew has dried but before the heat of the day.

Crab and Sage Bisque

Martha Gummersall Paul
Martha's Herbary
Pomfret, CT

Makes 6 servings

6 scallions, finely chopped
4 Tbsp. unsalted butter
1/3 cup flour
3 cups milk
1 1/2 cups half-and-half
2 tsp. salt
1/2 tsp. ground mace
1/2 tsp. paprika

3 Tbsp. chopped fresh
  sage (3 tsp. dried)
Tabasco to taste
1 lb. crabmeat, picked over
  for shell and cartilage
paprika for garnish
chopped fresh sage
  for garnish

1. Saute scallions in butter until softened, 3-4 minutes.
2. Blend in flour and cook over low heat for 5 minutes.
3. Stir in milk and half-and-half. Cook until just thickened.
4. Stir in spices, sage, and Tabasco. Mix well.
5. Fold in crabmeat. Heat gently, garnish with paprika and/or sage, and serve.

Fish Chowder

Linda E. Sampson Costa
Sampson's Herb Farm
East Bridgewater, MA

Makes 6 servings

- 1 large onion, chopped
- 1 Tbsp. butter
- 1 Tbsp. olive oil
- 2 cups water
- 1 large fresh or dried bay leaf
- 5 large potatoes, cut in small pieces
- 2 lbs. haddock or cod
- 10-12-oz. can evaporated milk
- 1/2 cup cream
- 2 Tbsp. flour
- freshly ground black pepper
- 2 tsp. chopped fresh thyme (2/3 tsp. dried)
- 2 tsp. salt

1. In heavy stockpot saute onions in butter and oil until translucent, about 10 minutes.
2. Stir in water, bay leaf, and potatoes. Simmer 10-15 minutes, until potatoes are almost soft.
3. Add fish to top of potatoes. Simmer for 7-8 minutes until fish flakes easily.
4. Add milk.
5. Mix together cream, flour, pepper, thyme, and salt. Add to potato/fish mixture and stir gently. Heat through and serve.

New England Clam Chowder

Stephanie L. Distler
Sweet Posie Herbary
Johnsonburg, PA

Makes 18 servings

- 1 lb. bacon, diced
- 3 celery stalks, diced
- 2 medium onions, diced
- 1 large carrot, diced
- 1/2 tsp. lovage seeds
- 1/2 cup butter or margarine
- 1 cup flour
- 3 quarts water
- 2 cups chicken stock
- 2 6-oz cans minced clams, with juice reserved
- 1 Tbsp. chopped fresh thyme (1 tsp. dried)
- 1 Tbsp. chopped fresh parsley (1 tsp. dried)
- 3 fresh or dry bay leaves
- 4 medium potatoes, diced
- 2 cups milk
- ground cayenne pepper (optional)

1. Saute bacon until almost crisp. Stir in celery, onions, carrots, and lovage seeds. Saute for 5 minutes.
2. Add butter. Stir until melted. Stir in flour.
3. Add water, chicken stock, clam juice (reserving clams), thyme, parsley, and bay leaves. Cover and simmer for 45-60 minutes.
4. Add potatoes. Simmer on medium heat for 10-15 minutes, or until potatoes are soft.
5. Add clams and simmer for 5 minutes.
6. Lower heat, pour in milk, and season with pepper.

Chicken Barley Soup

Candace Liccione
The Herbal Sanctuary
Royersford, PA

Makes 4 servings

de-boned chicken breast
2 quarts water
2 stalks celery, chopped
half a medium onion, chopped
2 carrots, chopped
1 leek, chopped
1/2 cup barley
coarse black pepper, to taste
1 Tbsp. chopped fresh thyme (1 tsp. dried)
1/4 cup chopped fresh parsley (5 tsp. dried)
2 Tbsp. chopped fresh sweet marjoram (2 tsp. dried)

1. Simmer chicken in water for 20 minutes. Remove meat and chop into bite-sized pieces.
2. Stir vegetables and barley into chicken broth and cook until barley is soft.
3. Add seasonings and herbs and bring to boiling point. Add chicken and serve.

Japanese Noodle Soup

Diane Tracey
Chestnut Herb Farm
North Ridgeville, OH

Makes 4 servings

6 cups vegetable broth
2 carrots, diced
2 celery stalks, diced
2 scallions, sliced
1 tsp. fresh dill or parsley

1 1/2 tsp. fresh thyme
(1/2 tsp. dried)
5 oz. Japanese bean noodles
or soy noodles
sea salt to taste

1. Bring broth to boil. Add carrots and celery. Cover and bring to boil. Reduce heat and simmer about 10 minutes, or until vegetables are almost tender.
2. Turn up heat and add scallions, dill or parsley, thyme, and noodles. Stir to break noodles apart. Simmer, covered, until noodles are done (about 3 minutes). Serve immediately.

Tip for Using Herbs

Shari Jensen
Crestline Enterprises
Fountain, CO

Always crush dry herb leaves just before adding them to your recipes. This action releases their oils.

Autumn Bisque

Kathy Hertzler
Lancaster, PA

Makes 6 servings

1 lb. butternut squash
2 tart apples, peeled, cored, and cubed
1 medium onion, chopped
2 slices white or wheat bread, crusts removed and cubed
4 cups chicken broth
1/2 tsp. salt
1/4 tsp. pepper
1 tsp. fresh rosemary (1/4 tsp. dried)
1 tsp. fresh marjoram (1/4 tsp. dried)
2 egg yolks beaten with 3/4 cup milk and 1/4 cup whipping cream
apple slices
fresh rosemary

1. Cut uncooked squash into quarters. Peel, seed, and cut into 1" cubes.
2. Combine squash, apples, onion, bread cubes, chicken broth, salt, pepper, rosemary, and marjoram in 4-quart saucepan. Bring to boil; then reduce heat and simmer uncovered for 35-40 minutes, or until squash and apples are tender. Remove from heat and cool slightly.
3. Spoon one-third of soup into blender container or food processor. Cover and blend or process until pureed. Repeat with remaining soup. Return to saucepan.
4. Reheat over low heat. Stir in milk mixture. Stir and heat just until it reaches the boiling point. Do not boil.
5. Garnish with apple slices and rosemary.

Harvest Stew

Jacqueline Swift
Rainbow's End Herbs
Perrysburg, NY

Makes 16 servings

1½ lbs. venison or beef stewing meat
1 Tbsp. olive oil
10 medium-sized fresh tomatoes, peeled and chopped
2 medium onions, chopped
1 clove garlic, minced
2 cups water
1 tsp. salt (optional)
6 medium potatoes, quartered
4 carrots, cut in 2" chunks
2 cups fresh corn
2 cups fresh green beans, cut
3 celery stalks, sliced
1 cup small summer squash, sliced
¼ cup snipped fresh parsley
freshly ground pepper

1. Brown meat in oil over medium-high heat.
2. Stir in tomatoes, onions, garlic, water, and salt. Bring to boil. Reduce heat, cover, and simmer for an hour.
3. Add potatoes, carrots, corn, green beans, and celery. Simmer 30 minutes more.
4. Stir in squash. Cook 10 more minutes.
5. Add parsley and fresh pepper.

Note: This soup freezes well.

Variation: In place of meat, substitute 1 lb. tofu mashed with soy sauce, oregano, and rolled oats. Brown, then add vegetables as directed above.

Rosemary Stew

Quailcrest Farm
Wooster, OH

Makes 4 servings

3 cups diced tomatoes	salt to taste
3/4 cup chopped celery	pepper to taste
1/2 cup chopped fresh parsley	1 1/2 lbs. stewing beef cubes
3/4 tsp. chopped fresh oregano	2 Tbsp. butter or margarine
(1/4 tsp. dried)	1 tsp. minced garlic
3/4 tsp. chopped fresh thyme	1/2 cup dry white wine
(1/4 tsp. dried)	1 Tbsp. fresh rosemary
2 Tbsp. olive oil	(1 tsp. dried)

1. Mix together tomatoes, celery, parsley, oregano, thyme, oil, salt, and pepper. Bring to boil. Simmer 30 minutes. Put through food mill and set sauce aside.
2. Trim excess fat from meat. Heat butter in skillet and cook beef until it loses its red color. Stir in garlic. Pour into greased casserole.
3. Add wine to skillet. Cook over high heat until reduced by half. Pour wine, tomato sauce, and rosemary over beef in casserole. Cover and bake at 300° for 2 hours, or until meat is tender.

About the Authors

Dawn J. Ranck is an advocate of bringing herbs to everyone's kitchens, not just to the cooking artists'.

A resident of Harrisonburg, Virginia, she is also the co-author of *A Quilter's Christmas Cookbook*.

Phyllis Pellman Good, Lancaster, Pennsylvania, has had her hand in many cookbooks—among them, *The Best of Amish Cooking, Recipes from Central Market,* and *The Best of Mennonite Fellowship Meals*.